Once Around Bullough's Pond

BOOKS BY DOUGLAS WORTH

Of Earth, 1974

Invisibilities, 1977

Triptych, 1979

From Dream, From Circumstance:
  New & Selected Poems, 1963–1983, 1984

Once Around Bullough's Pond, 1987

DOUGLAS WORTH

Once Around Bullough's Pond

A Native American Epic

William L. Bauhan, Publisher
DUBLIN, NEW HAMPSHIRE

Library of Congress Cataloguing in Publication Data:
Worth, Douglas.
Once around Bullough's Pond.
1. Indians of North America — Massachusetts — Poetry.   I. Title.
PS3573.069605   1987   811'.54   87-17876
ISBN 0-87233-092-3

This book was typeset in Linotron Bembo with
headings in Perpetua by TCI, Chicopee, Massachusetts,
printed at the Cabinet Press, Inc., Milford, New Hampshire,
and bound at the New Hampshire Bindery, Concord.
Wood engraving vignettes by Thomas Bewick.

Printed in the United States of America

Acknowledgments

The author would like to thank the Massachusetts Arts Lottery Council for a grant awarded in 1983 that helped him to complete this poem. Grateful acknowledgment to the editors of the following publications in which many of the sections of this poem first appeared:

Blue Unicorn: April 18, April 20, April 22
Earthwise Poetry Journal: April 10
Crab Creek Review: April 14
Poetic Justice: April 25
The Unknowns: April 4
The Charles E. Brown Newsletter: March 12
New Mexico Humanities Review: April 16
Whole Life Times: March 7, March 8
MAĀT: April 24, April 28, April 30, May 2
Reflections on the Sacred Gift of Life: April 6, April 8
Prophetic Voices: March 24
Electrum: March 2

To the memory of my parents
C. Brooke Worth
who introduced me to the wonders of Nature
and Merida Grey Worth
who encouraged my efforts in poetry

"It may be that some little root
of the sacred tree still lives.
Nourish it then, that it may leaf and bloom
and fill with singing birds."

—BLACK ELK

February: Prologue

February 25

Heart tremors. Chest pains diagnosed years ago
as nervous tension. A worrisome fuzz on my tongue
that doesn't get worse, but hasn't gone away, either,
in three years. Waking at four to lie and wrestle
with images: a ghostly flock of missiles
streaking toward me in moonlight; the blossom-littered
   casket
of the lovely infant daughter of good friends;
strewn piles of tenured colleagues being cut
right and left around me; breadlines stretching like
   flashbacks
to the 30's; millions of bloated third-world bellies
bursting with nothing; whole harvests rotting in silos;
the President flashing his million-dollar grin
as he hawks his new, streamlined military budget
   of 238 billion as "minimal."
Balding, beard splashed with silver, twenty pounds over
what I was when we moved from New York to
   Massachusetts
thirteen years ago, I take this middle-aged wreck
of a body, three or four times a week, after work,
barring colds or blizzards, and haul it out the front door
to jog with Rover up Grove Hill, onto Prospect,
down the hill, across Walnut, and once around Bullough's
   Pond.

And love it! God, it's good to get out, away,

for a few minutes, to feel yourself breathing, stretching,
an animal, running: bone, muscle, sinew, blood
all flowing together, moving you through a landscape
of slowly circling green, gold-crimson, brown, white,
along with redwings, mallards, turtles, squirrels
wheeling gulls, shrieking jays, the rattling cry
of a kingfisher, poised in midair, about to plunge,
the sound of traffic on Walnut quickly fading
to blend with the rush of water from the falls
that spills the pond into Smelt Brook, while above you
the sky's turning salmon, the trees holding out dim
    treasure,
as it must have been for the people living here
for thousands of years before we came bearing gifts:
trinkets, guns, booze, plagues, and the American dream
of plenty of land to make everyone rich, which, failing
to tempt them, brushed them aside or wiped them out . . .

Then back up Lakeview, panting, praying that Sam
the neighbors' Doberman's inside, turning up Grove Hill
and back through the crumbling picket fence into the yard
that a piece of paper we have calls Karen's and mine,
though really we're only sharing it for a time
with grass, flowers, shrubs, a few animals, birds and
    trees—
at any rate, "home," and ready for anything
from mastodons to the news to squalling kids
once I've showered and fixed myself a long, cold Scotch.

Bullough's! My God, what a stuffy, senseless name
for a place of such abiding loveliness
still blooming, wild, at the heart of civilization
despite everything: despite Bullough, city hall, me
who've cast around it a slowly tightening noose
of concrete, greed, and chemicals, closing in
but not yet cutting off its breath of life.

I wonder what its real name is—or the one
it had for thousands of years before we arrived
with our charters and wigs and arrogance and ambition
to build a new town and put Newton on the map—
Great Spirit's Eye? Gull's Wing? Kingfisher's Mirror?

Gulls still glide here, and kingfishers hover and dive,
though I've seen more fish floating dead than caught alive
by birds or the kids who still come to try their luck,
and if there's anything here that stands for me
as symbol, it's that hunched, gray, wading bird
who lurks in the reeds at pond's edge, reflecting, gazing
beneath the clouded surface, much as I
try to fathom the obscure soul of America,
in love still, skeptical, but not despairing—
poet and bird in an aging civilization
probing the murky waters of our times
for signs of hope, living images to sustain us.

February 28

Fenced off, with DANGER. THIN ICE. NO SKATING. signs.
The pond so polluted with salt and junk from the roads
it never froze over solidly this winter.
EMERGENCY PUBLIC TELEPHONE INSIDE
a little green box. But whom would I call to say
"The pond's dying. We're on thin ice. Come quick!
  Before
no one can skate here ever, or birds survive
the fish they catch, or fish the waters, or herons
find frogs or poets images of hope.
Before Newton's like that town the paper mentioned
one morning recently: Times Beach, Missouri,
that the current administration has offered to buy
after confirming it's so contaminated
with toxic dioxin, sprayed on the town's roads
for a decade or so, to keep the dust from blowing,
that it threatens the lives of everyone living there;
so the President's generously offered to relocate
all of the twenty-four hundred residents
that the EPA never bothered to warn, though it knew
for years what was happening?" It makes you wonder
what the Chief's got in mind for America
once the entire globe's lethal with radiation
from the holocaust he's assured us we could survive:
free seed packets, trowels, one-way tickets to the moon?

March

March 2

I found in the library, yesterday afternoon,
some stuff about the Native Americans
who lived in this region. Called the Massachusetts,
(which means "place of great hills"), they settled in small
  bands
near streams and ponds each spring and stayed through
  summer
fishing and hunting, planting beans and corn
"when the leaves of the white oak were big as the ears of a
  mouse,"
gathering roots and berries, nuts and herbs;
moving on in the fall to be close to the deer they hunted
through winter when they depended more on meat.
It said robbery and murder were rare among them
and that they lived, for the most part, peacefully,
and when tribes fought over hunting grounds or insults
it usually ended when the first brave got hurt;
that they were astonished when they battled the British
by how many could die in war; that it wasn't their custom
to take scalps till we offered to pay for them.
It said that women took part in village councils
and could leave their husbands anytime they chose.
It said stew was always simmering in a village
and no stranger, red or white, went away hungry.
It said they treated the spirits of all creatures,
among whom they lived as siblings, with respect,
begging forgiveness of the ones they killed,

wasting nothing, downing the flesh to the last morsel,
using the hide for clothes and moccasins,
sinew for bowstrings, horn and bone for tools.
It said they celebrated such festivals
as sugaring in March and planting in May
and made songs and spells and chants for every occasion
from warding off colds to making the corn grow tall,
often guided in this by their shaman, their medicine man,
who kept in touch with the spirits that dwell in all things,
created and overseen by the Great Spirit,
and who'd fast in times of calamity to appease
the angered spirits, and make lighter magic
to entertain and charm at other times.
It said they loved dancing and singing and storytelling,
having no written language, tales about tricksters
fables and myths, often spiced with humor and sex
which shocked the Puritan fathers who must have thought
they'd left behind such leanings with Shakespeare and
    Chaucer.
It said young men, courting, would sing or play their
    flutes
at their sweethearts' wigwams on sultry summer evenings
until they came out to stroll with them into the dusk.
Some grandfathers still, it said, would sing in the evenings
to their "mountain flowers," their lovely "spirit
    blossoms."
It said they played football, hockey, lacrosse, and handball,
gambled with painted pebbles, played cards made of rush,
kept dogs for pets, made popcorn and strawberry bread,
and overindulged their kids who grew sleek and saucy.

It said that before we brought in the idea of heaven
they had no conception of "happy hunting grounds,"
finding everything here as it should be. In short, it sounds
like a good life they led for millennia
till it came to a sudden end in the 1600's
through a series of battles and even more lethal plagues
brought over by white men, along with their thunder
    sticks,
that wiped out nine out of ten of the Massachusetts
in village after village, and scattered the rest.

March 4

Not that their lives were Edenic before we came,
exposed as they were to sudden storms and droughts,
epidemics, wild animals, wandering hostile tribes.
God knows I wouldn't want to have to move
each fall with the deer, or fend off wolves and bear
with stone-tipped arrows and spears—I've got my hands
    full
with Sam, after jogging, or on my way to the bus
in the morning, when he barks from his yard and comes
    charging,
fangs bared, as I keep on walking, scarcely breathing,
or stop with a prayer and croak out, "Good dog! Good
    Sam!"
never sure if the sniffing and licking he sometimes does
at my hand's being friendly or whetting his appetite
for the softer flesh of my throat! And the raccoons and
    skunks
I've surprised now and then at the trash cans at night have
    scared me
far more than I them, I'm sure; and even the squirrels
that plop from the roof to the bird feeder at the window
in the kitchen where I write have given me looks
that made me wonder which of us was at home.
So I'm not pushing the life of the "happy savage"
by any means. I'm grateful for supermarkets
where meals lie quietly wrapped in cellophane;
and where would I be without modern medicine,
having had scarlet fever as a child
and mumps at seventeen? Don't get me wrong—

I couldn't be more delighted with the triumphs
of civilization, from Mozart to central heating,
typewriters to ice cubes. But somewhere along the way
we seem to have lost something, some sense of perspective
and reverence toward nature, toward each other,
where we've come from, that we really are brothers and
    sisters
to animals, trees and streams, and that we need them
if we're to go on with our video games and computers,
our music of chance, our theater of the absurd,
because the bottom line is we've got to breathe
air and drink water and harvest food from the land,
and if we keep plundering, wasting, and poisoning them
with toxic dioxin, acid rain, radiation,
out of myopic selfishness and greed,
we're going to die, along with most everything else;
and maybe the people who lived here before us had
    something
that could help us, *save* us, though we nearly destroyed
    them:
some sense of the balance, the interconnectedness,
the complex harmony of the world, created
by some cosmic spirit greater than we can fathom
but that we can try to honor, as they did
before Lieutenant John Spring built the first grist mill
in Newton, on Smelt Brook in 1731
and cut off the fish that used to come up the Charles
from the ocean and fill Bullough's Pond each spring;
before Bullough, "the ancient proprietor of the land,"
put his shoulder to the profitable wheel
of progress when, quote, "this beautiful sheet of water,
like a sapphire gem set round with emeralds
(was) of tolerable depth and great purity."

March 7

Sometimes I imagine someone running before me,
ahead a few paces, and a few hundred years,
whose people had been around for several thousand,
who knew and loved this pond; someone like me
but younger, who used to circle the pond each day
two or three times, out of sheer exuberance,
in moccasins or barefoot, not having to worry
about shards of broken bottles and rusting cans;
who lived up the hill, as I do, with his wife
and kids and dog and neighbors, squirrels and skunks,
raccoons and flowers; someone like me, but fresher,
more brimmed with the juice of living, less skeptical
about his place and role in the universe;
a poet, no, bard! from whose breast song came gushing
pure and deep and clear and elemental
as blue sky, flaming maple, cardinal's whistle,
yet playful as the iridescent sheen
of a mallard's head spraying beads of sunlit water;
a singer-priest, highly honored in his village
by people living more simply in a time
when humans were closer to birds and trees and water
and profits were edible, and bits of seashell
were crafted and strung in patterns as gifts to wear:
wampum, before we dulled that term with trade.
I'd like to think someone of that sort really existed,
when America itself was younger, fresher,
and call his spirit back and get to know him
as I jog along in his footsteps, but how to address him?

March 8

Forerunner? Brother? Companion? What should I call you?
Running Wolf? Deerfoot?

                                      Bluefisher I am named
after the gray-blue bird who soars and hovers
above the fish-brimmed waters of this pond
we call Earth Mother's Basket, folds its wings
and like a spear-point plunges, disappears
with a splash below the surface, re-emerging
to climb the air again with silver treasure
clasped in its beak. My spirit too ascends
to hang with cloud or sun or moon or star
over the world, looking far and slow and deep
beneath the surface, into the souls of things,
sensing connections, seeing how wing and leaf,
bone and reed, star and flake, standing bear and brave
are woven into one pattern, cousins, children
of the Great Spirit Father and Earth Mother.
And when such vision fills me till I shiver
with awe, delight, and wonder, I too plunge
and, with a flash of inspiration, pierce
the world to its sacred essence, bringing forth
riches: songs, chants, prayers, stories, for my people,
for I am shaman, powaw, medicine man,
healer, priest, entertainer, singer, clown,
man-flute through whom creation's voices flow.

March 12

Little purple flowers, blooming so delicately
among curled leaves, shriveling patches of old snow,
how open and trusting you are, your arms thrown wide,
exposing the pure white innocence of your breasts,
the slender yellow stalks tipped with golden treasure.

Foolish blossoms, shaken by every breeze,
don't you know that Winter may pass this way again
and cloak you in ice and snow? And his friend the North
  Wind
snap your thin stems and scatter your pretty petals?

Rootless warrior-hunter, stepping so cautiously
in deerskin shoes among puddles and mounds of snow,
how closed and fearful you are of what you don't know.
We were here to welcome the Spirit of Spring
long before the first arrow shooters came,
and we will be here to praise the sweet buds of her breasts
long after the last, cruel, blood-encrusted stone
lies buried deep in the heart of Mother Earth.

Foolish human, if you would call yourself brave,
loosen your bow, cast off your shoes and robe,
fling your arms wide, and as your feet sink in mud
let the cool hands of Wind, the warm lips of Light
play over your breast and the treasure stalk you keep hidden
until you stand brimming, worthy to toast the slim spirit
approaching, dreamily, with sun-drunk sighs.

March 14

Old Stony Coat, ancient ice spirit, lying sprawled
in Earth Mother's Basket, half-asleep, get up!
Up, lazy bones, and head north where you belong
before Spring Spirit finds you drowsing here
and melts your icicle! Up now, drooling graybeard.
You've had the pond all winter. Now it's time
to loosen your cold embrace and let the sun
caress and stir her back to life. It's time
for Gull to bob and drift like a child's birch boat,
and Mallard, with his sweetheart, blissfully paddling,
in a sudden fit of passion, to plunge his head
into the water till only his ass sticks up,
then right himself, and, kicking, spread his wings,
flap furiously, and go whooshing across the surface
in a blur of sunlit spray and gleaming feathers—
while she, for whom this dazzling show's intended,
floats calmly on, demurely tucked, her tail
flicking from side to side to show she's seen
but doesn't think much of such male foolishness.
It's time for Redwing to build among the reeds,
and Oriole blaze, and Kingfisher freeze in air,
and Heron stare at his feet, and Bluejay jeer,
while Mockingbird pokes fun at everyone.
It's time for Fish to flash, and Frog to croak
his passion song at dusk, and time for Turtle
to sneak like a floating boulder around the pond.
It's time for Raccoon to scrub his delicate hands,

and Doe drop down her lovely neck to sip
at her reflection, and Bear scoop fish for lunch,
and Dragonfly, like a tiny, magic arrow
of flame or ice, dart two or three places at once.
It's time for me, the moist ground softening,
to run again, barefoot, round and round the pond,
until I hear Wind whispering in my hair
and feel the hearts of roots pounding under my feet,
blood climbing trunks, limbs stretching sleepy fingers;
round and round, until I am Moon and Sun
circling the Earth as I fly! Up, sluggish one.
Enough of your dull gray glinting. Take off! Scram!

March 16

Making maple sugar, or song, is good, hard work
of a not dissimilar kind. First you must tap
the life juice of a tree, and let it gather
slowly, watery tricklings; mumblings, hummings
only vaguely suggesting the essence of what's to come.

Then you dip the thin sap into a birch-bark kettle
and hang it over the glowing coals of a fire
to simmer for several days until it thickens
into a syrup; strings of notes and words
tumbling, regrouping, sorting, refining themselves.

Next you pour the syrup into a cooling trough
and knead it or stir it with a wooden paddle
until it is slow and creamy; savored phrases
beginning to align themselves with others,
jarring, grating, smoothing out, twining, blending.

At last you put the soft sugar into bark moulds
in the shapes of leaves or pine cones, and let it harden;
the stanzas set now, ready to be offered—
the sweet, sharp richness of the world, distilled,
flooding your mouth, setting flame to your throat, as you
    sing!

March 19

Rest assured, Little Brother, as you slowly turn
sizzling, we will waste nothing, savoring you
to the last morsel, sucking on every bone.

And when your flesh has become part of us,
we will preserve your lovely glossy coat
by turning it into a hat for our ears in winter.

The wonder of your ever-lengthening teeth
will be recalled for ages, as they click
strung on your sinew, handsomely set off by beads.

Nor will your bones lie idly whitening,
but will keep busy and useful as before
when you employed them: scraping, poking and digging.

Even the finer bits and claws will serve
to keep the children happily at their games
of counting and sorting, rainy afternoons.

Therefore, O Beaver, forgive us, if you can
for taking your life. The Great Spirit made it so
that creatures kill other creatures—but only in need.

A curse upon him who slaughters with pride for sport,
lugging the head home, leaving the carcass to rot!
Come, we will eat you now, properly, with respect.

March 21

Hail, Grinning Fox! Triumphant warrior
of the Massachusetts! You, who clasped the arm
of Courage, and spat in the face of Common Sense
when you flirted yesterday with the pretty wife
of Gray Wolf, who'd come to our village for a council
of neighboring sachems. Slitting your eyes at her
and flexing your muscles, until she had to cough
to hide her amusement, and the chief noticed you.

You, who took such offense when Gray Wolf smiled
at your idiocy and called you a fine young cub
which caused you to challenge him and all his braves
to battle, risking the lives and happiness
of many over a trifle.

                    You, who ducked
when the first arrow whistled over your head
and made your butt a target for Gray Wolf's practice,
escaping injury with more luck than cunning
by a feather's breadth, when your shirt was pinned to a tree
by a stray arrow; howling until we came
to free you, and one of our braves started whooping with
     laughter,
and Gray Wolf arrived and couldn't resist joining in,
then one after another, catching the fever,
we leaned on our bows, stamping helplessly, both sides
     collapsing,
thus ending, happily, the whole stupid affair.

Hail, fearless brave! Your grin is not so wide
as it was yesterday. Go now and grow
to be a man who thinks before he pokes
his tongue in a honeycomb. Go, Grinning Fox,
with your head up, lest we rename you Slinking Dog!

March 23

Out fighting with Grinning Fox the other day
to try to rescue the young brave's kidnapped pride,
Mild Muskrat caught a cold, or a cold caught him
as it often does when he overexerts himself,
having, from birth, been delicate, though strong
with a power of gentleness in his hands and voice
for easing the backs and smoothing the ruffled feathers
of many an aching brave or angered neighbor.

Therefore, O Streaming Nose, potent spirit of colds,
bold scratcher of throats, mightly piler of phlegm in the
    chest,
ease up on Mild Muskrat, let him once again breathe
comfortably through the night beside his wife
instead of waking up clogged and coughing his lungs out
until she jerks the bearskin over her head
and contemplates murder or moving back in with her
    folks.

Look, I have put on my shaman's robe and the mask
with the foot-long, flaming nose, and the eyes gunked
    shut,
and pounded my drum like a headache's throb as I danced
three times around the village, hacking and sneezing,
to remind my people of your terrible powers
and beg you to relent and leave Mild Muskrat
in peace. If you must plague someone in our village
take Grinning Fox, who so juicily deserves you,
and like you, O Spirit, has proven himself at running!

33

March 24

Sly Dog, you shameless trickster, beggar, thief,
sniffing around the stewpot at dinner time
as if you just happened to be passing by
tracking a rabbit or squirrel, and suddenly lost it
and figured it must have leapt up into the stew.
And when we sit to eat, plunking your head
in our laps like a gift, looking up with such pleading eyes,
such twitching of eyebrows, high-pitched, mournful
    whines,
we throw you a morsel just to get rid of you
for a moment and try to enjoy our meal in peace.

And if there's no food to be had, it's affection you're after
as if we'd nothing better to do all day
than pet you, eternally stroking, patting and scratching,
pawing at us while we're busy with our tasks,
burrowing under a hand with your cold wet nose
so we upset the bead dish or slice ourselves fixing stew,
and if we've lain down for a little rest, sneaking up
to drench our ears with your slobbery, slug-like tongue,
or dropping a stick on our unprotected faces
and yapping furiously for us to get up
to throw it so you can bring it back again.

Then at night, when you're supposed to be on guard
outside the wigwam, snoring obliviously
while bears swarm by or raccoons scatter our stores,
then waking an hour before dawn when we're still asleep
and baying at some imaginary intruder

because you're lonely, and then, when we let you in,
thumping and snuffling and licking until we go crazy
and throw you out again to bark some more.

O terror of ticks and fleas, we'd be better off
without your smelly carcass poking about—
and yet, last week, when you didn't show up at dinner
and we ate in strange peace and quiet, and you still hadn't
 come
when we closed up the wigwam and lay down to sleep . . .
we couldn't, all of us breathing quietly,
listening for your sharp yap, the quick dance of your paws
until I got up and went out to search for you
all around the pond, up and down the glimmering brook,
and came back without you and lay down again
hearing the thump of my heart, the restless turning
of Running Deer and Little Squirrel, the sighs
of Goldwing, Cooing Dove squalling in fits till dawn . . .
when you arrived, softly whimpering, on three paws,
blood crusting your neck and muzzle, stinking of swamp,
and, cursing and crooning, we stroked you, gently, and
 kissed you,
and fed you out of the stewpot and bathed your wounds
and wrapped you in blankets and set you on our best
 bearskin,
and you sat there, yapping and grinning, you terrible
 creature,
sassy and proud as a brave who comes staggering
home after his first battle or night of love.

March 26

Once Porcupine had the softest coat of all.
If you don't believe me, tickle him under the chin
until he rolls over and stretches out on his back;
then stroke his belly—you'll find that it's even softer
than Rabbit or Mole. A long, long time ago
his coat was like that all over, so tempting to stroke
that nobody who came near him could resist,
including Chief War Cloud's daughter, the lovely
   sweetheart
of True Arrow, a fierce young brave in the tribe.
Sparkling as stones in water were the eyes
of Laughing Brook, and sweet as maple syrup
her flowing voice, and she had quite a body, too!
And True Arrow was jealous, crazy jealous
of anyone who even looked at her.

One day, when she was passing Porcupine
who was lying stretched in the sun, she stooped to stroke
his lovely coat, but True Arrow seized her wrist
and vowed he would murder Porcupine if she ever
touched him again. Poor Porky was terrified
and furious, complaining it wasn't his fault
that everyone liked to stroke him. Well, sure enough,
it happened—one day when she thought no one was
   looking
Laughing Brook brushed her hand down Porcupine's back
as she passed him at the pond. True Arrow's spy,
Raven, observing this, flew croaking away.
Luckily for Porcupine, his friend Sparrow

saw Raven spying on Laughing Brook and followed
and saw True Arrow gathering all his friends
to come and shoot Porky. When the poor creature heard,
he fled to the woods, but True Arrow tracked him down
and he and his friends enclosed him in a tight circle
all pointing their arrows at him. "Mercy!" he cried.
"Great Spirit, don't let them kill me. Is it my fault
that everyone likes to stroke me? Help me, please!"
True Arrow's heart was quartz, but the Great Spirit,
who happened to be looking that way from the sky,
heard Porcupine, and, softened with compassion,
decided to do what he could. He couldn't change
True Arrow's nature, having created him so,
but as the brave cried out, "Shoot!" and bowstrings
    twanged,
he turned the arrows, just as they reached their mark,
so that the feathered ends slid into Porcupine
without killing him and lodged with their points sticking
    out.

And ever since that day Porcupine's gone about
with arrows bristling all over his back and tail.
(They missed his head and neck, which he'd tucked under
as True Arrow's friends let fly. And the tips have worn
    down,
from rubbing against each other for thousands of years,
to the finest needle points.) So no one can stroke him,
unless, as I said, you tickle him under the chin
and he rolls over, belly up. But please don't try it,
you little ones, unless your mother or father
says it's O.K., and you ask him first, politely,
if he *wants* to be tickled. I'd hate for you to end up
with a quiver of arrows sticking out of your hand!

March 28

It's raining again. Running Deer and Little Squirrel
are sitting inside the entrance flap of the wigwam,
Running Deer drawing with a bone on bark
while her younger brother arranges small, smooth pebbles
in patterns. "What are you drawing?" asks Little Squirrel
in a tone that suggests he doesn't want to know
except to criticize. "Is it a caribou?"
As Running Deer says nothing, Little Squirrel
remarks, "Well, it doesn't look like a caribou."
Running Deer goes on drawing. "It looks like a dog
that is trying to be a moose." Little Squirrel laughs.
Running Deer still doesn't answer, though a line forms
between her eyebrows and she works her tongue
harder against her cheek as she goes on drawing.
Then a smile quietly blossoms across her face.
"If Daddy brought back nine deer eight days in a row
how many would we have?" Little Squirrel stops
the pattern he was working on and thinks,
scooping some pebbles up and shaking them
so they rattle in the hollow drum of his hands.
"Eighty-nine?" "Wrong! I thought you were so good
at numbers." "I am," he says, "for someone my age.
Ask me another." "No," she says, "you're too dumb.
You'd just get that one wrong too." "No I wouldn't," he
    says.
"You're just being mean to me because you're jealous
that everyone says how good I am at numbers

and you're not good at anything at all.
You can't even draw a caribou—look at that!"
"It's not supposed to be a caribou,
dummy—it's an imaginary creature
that can fly, and has horns made of candy, and eats little
    boys
who try to break off a piece." While Little Squirrel
takes all this in, carefully studying it, in silence,
he spreads out his pebbles in several short, neat rows.
"Seventy-two," he says, after a while.
"What flavor candy?" "Strawberry," Running Deer says,
"but it's poisoned, just in case some boy like you
breaks off a piece while it's sleeping and runs away.
You'd die a horrible death, turning blue in the face
and throwing up globs of green yuck all over the place,
just like you did the other night on your bearskin.
And while you were dying, we'd all laugh and laugh
at your stupid green face." "You just said it would be
    blue.
You're the stupid one. You're so dumb you can't
    remember
if something's blue or green. Mommy says you're dumb;
I heard her the other night talking to Daddy about it.
I bet you're the stupidest girl in the whole Massachusetts,
and you don't even have a you-know-what!" "A what?"
"A you-know-what. Down there. Like me and Raven."
"Girls aren't supposed to have them, pigeon-brain,
which shows how smart you are! I bet you think
they're just for making peepee, don't you? Hah!"
"I know what they're for," says Little Squirrel, softly.

"Tell me then. What? Go on. See? You don't know.
Well, they're for making babies!" Little Squirrel
arranges the pebbles into two long lines
next to each other, and answers, "No they're not.
You're just trying to trick me. Women make babies
in their bellies. I've seen them. Like Mommy did this
    winter
with Cooing Dove . . . Hey look, the sun's come out.
Come on, I'll race you down to the pond." "O.K.,
if you'll give me a headstart. Wait, no fair! Come back!"

March 30

Come, Long Nose, children snatcher. Here are two
prime victims: Running Deer and Little Squirrel
who've been squabbling and whining, clawing and
    bickering
since dawn over who goes first or who got more,
who's smarter, who's stronger, which one the dog likes
    better,
pestering Goldwing for sweets while she's making stew,
tearing in, shrieking, just as Cooing Dove
has gotten to sleep so she starts up screaming again,
sneaking off with my medicine rattle and drum
when only last week they carelessly broke my bone
    whistle
and left my best rattle lying exposed in the rain
that came down all afternoon and ruined it.

Come, nightmare spirit, friend to desperate parents.
These two I have here by the ears have been asking for you
to come and pop them into your big pack basket
and carry them off to your dark cave in the woods
and throw them into your bubbling pot and boil them
till all their nasty selfishness is cooked out
and they're ready to be gobbled up limb by limb
till only their bones, hair, nails and teeth are left.
Let's see if they're still arguing then as to which
is tenderer, tastes better, gets to your stomach first!
Here, take them, if you can stand them, and good eating!
I only hope they'll give you less indigestion
than they've given me, today, these two spoiled brats!

April

April 2

Still awake? It's late. No more talking now. Time to sleep.
A backrub? Well, all right. A very quick one. Move over.
It's funny, hearing the two of you laughing just now
reminded me of a time when I was your age
and played a trick on my sister, your Auntie Willow.
One evening, when she had gone out of the wigwam
to wash up for the night, I put a big frog
way down at the foot of her bearskin. When she came in
I tried to cover my laughter with a loud yawn
as I went out to wash up myself. We used to fight
and tease each other at least as much as you two
and Grandmother and Grandfather would get furious
and yell and scold us about how bad we were
and then forgive us. Anyway, when I came back
and got into bed, I lay very still in the dark
waiting for Willow to scream (She didn't like frogs
and hated to be surprised.)—but nothing happened.
"Willow," I said at last, unable to stand it
any longer, "Are you asleep?" "No," she replied.
Are you?" "Now how could I be talking to you
if I was asleep?" I said. She only giggled.
"Are you comfortable?" I said. "Uh huh," she answered.
"You know," I said, "I like to sleep with my feet
way down at the very bottom. Have you tried that?"
"That's how I always sleep," she said. "Oh," I said.
"Don't you like to wiggle your toes all around down there
and poke them into the corners?" "Yes," she said.

"Let's do it now, O.K.?" "O.K.," she said.
"It's fun," I said, "isn't it?" "Yes," she said, and giggled.
"Haven't you sometimes imagined something's down
   there
clammy and cold and horrible waiting to bite you?"
"I used to," she said, "but now I check down there first
before I get in, to be sure." "You do?" I said.
"Yes, always," she said. "Like tonight, you won't believe
what I found down there?" "You found something?"
   I said.
"Yes, an old frog. I guess it must have hopped in
when Mommy was airing the wigwam this afternoon."
"Oh," I said casually. "What did you do with it?"
"I let it go, of course, stupid!" she replied.
"Good," I said. "Well, goodnight." And feeling foolish
I turned over on my side and closed my eyes.
"Bluefisher?" she said, after a moment's silence.
"Are you asleep yet?" "No," I said. "What is it?"
"Do you ever sleep on your side with both hands tucked
under the pillow, nestling all cozy and warm?"
"Sometimes," I said. "Are you doing it now?" she asked.
"No," I said. "Try it," she said, and let out a squeak,
then a muffled whoop, and even before my hands
started moving up and under, I knew what I'd find.

April 4

Cooing Dove, coo, and I will give you the sun
to hold in your hand and toss high into the air
so that wherever you go will be light and warmth
and your life will be long and worthy. Cooing Dove, coo.

Cooing Dove, coo, and I will give you the moon
on a string of stars to wear round your neck like a shell
so that wherever you go a soft beauty will glow
and your life will be long and worthy. Cooing Dove, coo.

Cooing Dove, coo, and I will give you the wind
that is sighing for love, to billow your skirt and your hair
so that wherever you go men's hearts will be full
and your life will be long and worthy. Cooing Dove, coo.

Cooing Dove, coo, and I will give you the rain
that is weeping, weeping for all the sad things that happen
so that wherever you go will be eased by compassion
and your life will be long and worthy. Cooing Dove, coo.

Cooing Dove, coo, and I will give you the earth
to live on with all your brother and sister creatures
so that wherever you go you will be at home
and your life will be long and worthy. Cooing Dove, coo.

April 6

To dance the spring leaf, you must be darkness furled
upon itself, for months, then slowly, slowly
feel something deep within yourself begin
to stir, swell, tighten, start to edge its way
outward, toward something dimly felt, disturbing,
intriguing, drawing you further, gently insistent,
compelling, growing sharper till you ache
to stretch, spread, open, give yourself completely
into some softly flowing golden warmth
coaxing, caressing you, until you can't bear it
and burst forth, terrified, into the searing light
crying out something indistinct, over and over
whose meaning you can't quite grasp, but which you keep
   trying
more and more boldly: green, green! Green, GREEN!
   GREEN!

April 8

Each day some new wonder bursts upon the scene:
a miniature sun, a bush in purple flames,
a scarlet flash, a golden curl of song,
a rock at stream's edge robed in green, the smell
of rain one night announcing Spring's arrival.

In the village girls rub bear fat into their hair
till it shines in the sun like water; their young breasts,
swelling out, tilt more sharply, tender nipples
darkened and tight with blood. The first warm evening
Grandfather sits and croons to his chickadee
whose cap has gone gray, while Mother shakes her head
and glances at Father sideways. The merciless young
bicker and whine at bedtime, then sneak out
to probe the pond for frogs, the shadows for lovers,
while the not quite grown lie aching or stroke their way
halfway to the stars on single, shuddering wings.

One morning, lifeless all winter, the pond explodes!

April 10

The sun is chief of nature's glorious circles
most would agree, though some might pick the moon
as being more refined—but when you stand
before me, naked, in all your natural splendor,
your eyes, your breasts, the soft round of your belly
are subtler than the moon, yet fire my blood
as no summer sun at midday ever could.

Its juicy tartness makes the raspberry
the perfect berry, some insist, though many
prefer the strawberry for its milder sweetness;
but to my tongue the most delectable
are those that swell to ripeness at the tips
of your full breasts and last from season to season.

A dove's the dearest thing alive, some say;
others a chipmunk; others a six-weeks puppy;
but I love the shy, little creature who makes its home
in that clump of brush on the mound below your belly
and pokes out its head when I go hunting there
and, growing bold and friendly, wants to play,
pressing against my fingers to be stroked
gently, at first, but more and more eagerly
until it's so filled with pleasure it brims over
in wave after wave of ecstasy, slowing subsiding,
withdrawing into its burrow, tender, sleepy,
saying, "So long. Drop by again, sometime."

Some swear a bear cave's the most dangerous
place to enter; others the woods in winter
when wolves are roaming in packs—but I would choose
the dark, mysterious tunnel between your thighs
where, groping blindly, I inch my cautious way
inward, the dank walls collapsing all around me,
retreating, plunging onward, deeper and deeper,
until I rouse the wild beast of your passion
and we lock and wrestle till the sweat pours from us
and, gasping and groaning, we can't tell if our hearts
are about to burst or blossom as we come,
shuddering, face to face with the Spirit of Love.

April 11

When, swollen with desire, I drop my robe
and strut before her, gut sucked flat as a drum,
cocking one eyebrow, singing a passion song
as if I were the Great Spirit himself
courting Mother Earth . . .

                   and she, my sweet thorn-flower,
my sugar-arrow, her lovely face downturned,
tucks her small feet more neatly under her thighs,
fixes a flawless braid, untwining, twining,
goes on sorting beads, or slicing meat for stew
as if I were not there . . .

               so that I droop
and, turning, slink about like a skunked dog,
a raccoon caught in the rain, a shapeless scrap
of shell unfit for ankle, wrist or neck,
and brush the dust from my robe . . .

                      until she sighs,
and, laughing, lifts the shadows from her eyes
that say, "All right, you idiot man, come on!"
and opens to me . . .

             O then I rise in glory
like sun at morning, streaming everywhere,
warming her hills and meadows in a flood
of radiance, brimming, bursting . . .

                    Afterwards,
lying so quiet we can hear the leaves
uncurling above us, it seems to me our love
is a perfect blossom floating endlessly
on shell-smooth water, and I can't imagine
how it could ever be otherwise with us . . .

as sometimes, when I'm boastful, or forget
to do something I'd promised, or let slip
some thoughtless phrase that wounds or rouses her
to anger or contempt, and all my words
of excuse or explanation are like salmon
rising to torchlight and the flash of spears.

April 14

Greetings, pale one, you who came to our village
yesterday, uninvited, out of the blue
with one who speaks both our tongues, to hold a council,
and ate our stew and eyed our children's bare bodies
with wrinkled brow—you who had wrapped yourself
in layers of black despite the balmy day
and wiped sweat from your forehead constantly—
and looked upon our women's sun-bronzed breasts
with something more than shock or disapproval,
and when I sang one of our ancient spring songs,
in which Father Sky makes love to Mother Earth,
to honor and entertain you, squirmed as if
you'd sat on a swarming ant hill. You who brought
the thing you call a book, black as your robe
and filled with thin, dead, worm-infested leaves
you said contain the silent words of God,
who is a spirit greater than any of ours
like Long Nose or Stony Coat, or she whose breasts are
    blossoms,
greater, even, than the Great Spirit himself,
and the only spirit, all powerful, who created
everything, and causes all things to happen
and loves all people, even us who don't know him,
but is jealous of our spirits which we must give up,
and wants us to do this and not do that,
work hard all day and cover our women and children,
and if we do as he wishes will reward us

by sending us somewhere beyond the clouds called Heaven
when we die, where we will be nice and smile all day
forever, even though our mouths start to ache,
but if we disobey him will punish us
with sickness, maybe (and it's true we've heard
of other villages visited by white men
that were wiped out soon afterwards by disease)
and when we die throw us into a pit of flames
called Hell to roast forever but never cook;
and that what this God wanted us to do
right then and there was to get down on our knees
and hold the book in our hands and bend our heads
to kiss its blackness while you placed your hands
on our heads, one by one, and mumbled words
that made no sense to us—and so we did,
out of politeness and custom not to offend
a guest in our village, and also as a precaution
just in case all the things you said were true,
and out of respect for the magic thunder stick
you carried slung on your shoulder, which we have heard
is more powerful than a hundred arrows or spears
and has killed more than one brave who quarreled with
    white men.

We have discussed these matters most of the night
in our village council, and I, Bluefisher, was sent
to greet you, White Brother, and give you our best
    thoughts.
What good is this God of yours if you can't skin him
and cut him up for a stew and wear his coat,

or tremble at his great beauty, or plant his seed
to grow succotash, or put on his ugly face
to make the children behave or laugh at his pranks?
And if your God is so all powerful
and loves us, as you say, why did he allow
Death to come up through the underground wigwam's
    smoke hole?
and why does he let sickness kill innocent babies?
and evil men triumph in battle over good ones?
No, pale one, we prefer to keep our spirits
who seem more real and make more sense to us;
and if sickness spreads through our village, as it has
before, I will fast and chant and dance and pray
till the angered spirit who caused it is satisfied
and leaves us alone. You keep your one God—here
I've brought back your book—we'd rather kiss each other
than its cold blackness—when I felt your hands,
pale, veined with darkness, pressing down on my head
a chill ran through me, and I had a vision
that I was sinking slowly into a pit
cradled by some dark spirit—the Spirit of Death!

April 16

Lumbering Brother, if you have any sense,
you'll stay away from our village tonight. Should you
  come
sniffing and pawing around our syrup pots
and smoked meats again, you can expect a welcome
you won't soon forget if you're lucky enough to escape
being turned into a blanket for some brave's sweetheart.

And if you somehow survive our arrows and spears
we've something even more horrible planned for you:
we'll call on the white man's God to go after you
and catch you and quietly ask you to sit down
while he lectures you solemnly for three or four hours
till you're weeping from boredom and your rear end aches
about how you should do this and shouldn't do that
and how you must get down on your knees and beg
his forgiveness for everything you've ever done
that was evil, though you didn't know it was
and thought it was the natural thing to do;
and if you don't agree to everything
he says, he'll take his terrible thunder stick
and shove it up your ass and blast you to Hell!

April 18

In my dream I heard a voice out of the sky
calling me to arise. I spread my arms
and flew high, very high, past many clouds
until I saw a huge bird hovering
its vast wings stretching, cloudy white and blue,
clear across the sky. It called me, "Bluefisher,
why do you sit and sing when there are wolves
gathering in the woods, their snowy coats
bristling, their black jaws drooling, frothed with red?"
"I didn't know," I said. "Great Spirit, help me.
Tell me what I must do to save my people."
The voice said nothing further, but I saw
the great wings shrink till they became a man
who ran away singing, leading a band of people
across the sky, pursued by many wolves
howling and leaping at them; their snapping jaws
were black books dripping worms. As the people ran
they were dropping seeds of beans and corn, and I
ran after them, catching the seeds. The people vanished
and I flew down to earth to find the wigwams
around Earth Mother's Basket gone. I knelt
and wept for my people, beating my fists on the ground,
then felt the seeds I had caught. I opened my hands
and there were Running Deer, Goldwing, Little Squirrel
and all my people, looking up at me,
dancing and singing. This is what they sang:
"Remember the Massachusetts, we who sleep.

Remember the Massachusetts, planted deep."
So I got a sharp stick and dug many holes
all around the pond and planted my seed-people there.
And then I woke and found it was a dream,
but whether power dream or prophecy
I can't say, and I don't know what to do.

April 20

Drummer of thunder, hurler of lightning, hear
O hear the prayers of my people. It has rained
off and on almost every day this spring
so that we've sat inside, the old ones grumbling
about their aches and pains, the children bored
and at each other's throats. This morning Goldwing,
usually so mild and patient, slapped Little Squirrel
for teasing Running Deer, and later on
threw me out of the wigwam when I crept up
behind her as she was sweeping and threw my arms
around her waist and squeezed her. Enough, moist spirit
of soggy robes and drizzle. Though we pray
for you to come to us in times of drought,
you've gone too far—if you keep up like this
you'll rot the beans and corn we're about to plant—
even the fish in the pond have started complaining
that the water tastes too thin with all this rain!
Some say it is the white man's gloomy God
who has darkened the sky this spring, but I don't believe it.
I think you're just working too hard, and need a break.
Why don't you suck in your breath and draw up the fog
that hangs over Earth Mother's Basket like a cloak
and take a few days vacation, somewhere to the south
(but not too far, as we'll need you soon again)
and give brother Sun his turn to come out and play?

April 22

A day like the first day: sparkling, flawless, fresh
from the Great Spirit's fingers, just before
he set the world in motion. Blue so deep
it takes you to where beginning and end join hands
forever. Blossoming boughs hang breathlessly
like falls of frozen foam. Awash in light,
you feel as if you could do anything
you chose, but what you choose is to do nothing
but bloom in quiet warmth and sunlit wonder
while songbirds, waking, drowsily rehearse
their notes of joy and grief, and far above
silver wings hover, held by threads so fine
you can barely feel them snap as the creator,
drawing back, speaks the hushed command: "Begin!"

April 24

Hear us, O Hobbamock, and spare your people.

Spirit of greatest evil—famine, drought, flood,
fire, pestilence—it's been many years
since I called to you, dancing in moonlight around the fire,
shaking my rattle, yelling, twisting and writhing,
singing, praying and chanting, while my people
sing with me, throwing their beads and moccasins,
the new clothes they've worked on all winter, cutting and
    sewing,
into the blazing flames as offerings
to your great powers, begging you to relent.

Hear us, O Hobbamock, and spare your people.

Spirit whose touch is agony, hear me now
as I fall down and moan and cover myself with ashes.
Forgive us for what we've done to anger you.
Was it our bowing to the white man's God
who mumbles from that black book? We have cast him
    out
and will not let him into our village again.

Hear us, O Hobbamock, and spare your people.

Whatever our foolish deeds, we pray, we beg you:
accept these many gifts and take away

this new disease that is spreading through the village
like fire through the woods in early autumn.
Already, just two days since the first small sparks,
many are sick and some are clearly dying,
burning up, covered with dark red streaks and blotches,
pus breaking out all over their bodies and faces,
and none of my roots or herbs or healing songs help.

Hear us, O Hobbamock, and spare your people.

Hobbamock, we are dust if you say, "Die!"
Flowers blooming in sunlight if you say, "Live!"
O let us live so that we can honor you
for as long as leaves sprout green in spring, and turn
gold and scarlet in autumn. Take away
this terrible sickness from our beloved grandmothers
and grandfathers who deserve to die in peace.
Lift the flames of your fingers from our small children
who have barely begun their lives—spare Trickling Water
and Squirming Trout, Slow Turtle, and Cooing Dove,
whose tiny hands can have done nothing to offend you,
and yet who can't eat or sleep now, screaming and
    screaming . . .

Hear us, O Hobbamock, and spare your people.

April 25

The sky tonight is like a frosty web,
the moon a spider. Fly, my little dove,
to where sweet peace awaits you. Let my drum
steady your softly beating spirit wings.

Here for a season, you will never see
how blossoms fall before the fruits are ripe;
how fruits give way to a brief blaze of leaves
then bare sticks shaking in the bitter wind.

Forgive our tears at parting. Death, who takes
our loved ones from us, gives them back to keep
planted inside us, blooming quietly
as stars at evening. Rise now, turn away

and fly, fly onward, gladly; look ahead
to where a crowd, dear Grandmother among them,
is waiting to welcome you. Look, there she is
waving and smiling. That's it. Faster! Fly!

We won't be far behind you. Fly! Fly! Fly!

April 28

I have fasted four days and stayed awake four nights
chanting and smoking the pipe with the eagle feather
whose rising plumes make a bridge between earth and sky,
awaiting a power vision, some sign to show me
a way to save my people. Nothing came.
Nothing. No voice, no image, from the sky.
Nothing. While my people are dying around me.

Great Spirit, have you abandoned the Massachusetts,
enraged at our kneeling to the white man's God?
Or has that pale spirit triumped over you?
Forgive my suggesting it, but a shaman speaks truth,
or what he knows of truth, or his words are worthless.

Is it possible that this God, who scowls from the sky
at the loveliness of the body he created,
this God, who never laughs or thinks up tricks
to amuse his people, this scolding, jealous God
who's so greedy he wants to be the only one
and have everybody kneel down and worship him
and be serious, working from dawn to dusk every day,
and never tell dirty jokes . . . is it possible
that this passionless spirit's more powerful than you?

Great Spirit, if all the pale one said was true,
and that is why so many are sick and dying,
I think my people would rather die than serve

such a joyless spirit who has no lips to kiss
or arms to hug or sex to offer as gift
over and over again to the beloved
as flowers unfolding or rain pouring down from the sky.

Great Spirit, rather than live the white man's way,
I think we'd prefer to try the skewers of Hell
where, as we sizzled and dripped through eternity,
at least we'd be free of that maddening drone of advice
and could admire each other's nakedness.

It is the same in every village now,
The Massachusetts are dying. I've put away
my rattle and drum, my herbs. The Massachusetts
are dying. Running Deer and Little Squirrel
buried yesterday, The Massachusetts are dying.
Everywhere packing and burning. The Massachusetts
are dying. Tomorrow what's left of the village will go.
The Massachusetts are dying. Goldwing is burning,
her body stinking with pus. The Massachusetts
are dying. I, too, am dying; there is blood
and shit on my bearskin. The Massachusetts are dying.
There will be no planting of beans and corn this year.
The Massachusetts are dying. My people instead
are being planted, as in the prophecy
of the dream I had. The Massachusetts are dying.
Farewell, Earth Mother's Basket. Your fish must fill
other people's bellies. The Massachusetts are dying.
May the pale ones, if they come to live by your banks,
learn to love and respect your animals, birds, trees, fish
and flowers, as we did. The Massachusetts are dying.
May they swim in your waters and run around your edge.
The Massachusetts are dying. And years from now
some other singer celebrate your beauty.
The Massachusetts are dying. And think of me
long ago, weaving my stories, chants, legends and songs.
The Massachusetts are dying. So that my people
like seeds in spring will poke up their sleepy heads
and blossom again. The Massachusetts are dying.

May: Farewell

May 2

Farewell, Bluefisher. May your crumbling bones
some three hundred and fifty years ago
have fed the soil that fed the worm that slipped
from the hook to feed the fish that was caught by the
    gray-blue
great, great, ever-so-great grandfather
of the bird that inspired me to imagine you.

And may what I've written about you and your people,
though largely invention and most likely wrong
in many particulars, be true in spirit,
fact and imagination intertwining
as corn and beans growing together, the delicate vines
winding their blossoms around the sturdier stalks.

And may the reach and grandeur of your vision,
the flash of your wit, your insight's plunge and shock,
inspire me to make light of my bodily ills,
anxieties and frustrations, and breathe more deeply
as I circle Earth Mother's Basket, lifting my head
from brooding upon this self-destructive age
to rise up and gaze with you all ways at once
until I can feel the passionate dancing of atoms
in flowers and stars, vast galaxies spreading their petals,
and glimpse, in awe and wonder, the great design,
the brother-and-sisterhood of all creation
in which there are no strangers or enemies,

just creatures, linked in one cosmic family,
caught up together, whirling through space and time.

And may the spirit of the first Massachusetts,
reverent, joyous, springing up again
to live in these poems, tempt my people to dream
of a common wealth that has less to do with profits
than living in peace on a globe where nobody's starving,
honoring Mother Earth with love and respect—
instead of choking, stripping, mass raping her
and leaving her to die, as we seem to be doing—
celebrating her rhythms of sun and rain,
seeding and harvesting, bud and blossom and fruit,
while the Great Spirit hovers over all
rejoicing in the variousness of his children:
fur, skin, bark, scale, feather; laughing features
of red and yellow, brown and black and white—
a dream that seems flickering, fading, ever-receding,
that could save us, still, if we'd let it; a dream that once
was true, or truer, and isn't over yet.